FunTime® Piano

Hymns

Level 3A–3B

Easy Piano

Arranged by

Nancy and Randall Faber

Production: Frank and Gail Hackinson
Production Coordinator: Marilyn Cole
Cover: Terpstra Design, San Francisco
Music Editor: Edwin McLean
Engraving: Music Craft of Hollywood, Inc. (Fla.)

FABER
PIANO ADVENTURES®
3042 Creek Drive
Ann Arbor, Michigan 48108

A NOTE TO TEACHERS

FunTime® Piano Hymns is a collection of favorite hymns and spirituals arranged for the Level 3 pianist. Keys include C, G, F, and D Major, along with D and A Minor. The teachers may assign the pieces in the order given or may skip among selections, choosing by student interest.

FunTime® Piano Hymns is part of the *FunTime® Piano* series arranged by Faber and Faber. "FunTime" designates Level 3 of the *PreTime® to BigTime® Piano Supplementary Library*.

Following are the levels of the supplementary library, which lead from *PreTime®* to *BigTime®*.

PreTime® Piano	(Primer Level)
PlayTime® Piano	(Level 1)
ShowTime® Piano	(Level 2A)
ChordTime® Piano	(Level 2B)
FunTime® Piano	(Level 3A – 3B)
BigTime® Piano	(Level 4)

Each level offers books in a variety of styles, making it possible for the teacher to offer stimulating material for every student. For a complimentary detailed listing, e-mail faber@pianoadventures.com or write us at the mailing address below.

Visit **www.PianoAdventures.com**.

Helpful Hints:

1. Skillful pedaling is important in hymn playing. Pedal markings are provided in each piece. The student can benefit from practicing the left hand alone with attention to pedaling.

2. For a special project, the student may wish to record a selection of hymns and spirituals as a surprise gift for parents or grandparents.

3. Encourage students and parents to seek out opportunities for informal performances of hymns and spirituals, e.g., before or after a church choir rehearsal, for junior church service or Sunday School, or in a relaxed family gathering. Hymns are to sing and enjoy!

ISBN 978-1-61677-033-4

TABLE OF CONTENTS

Saviour, Like a Shepherd Lead Us 4

Jesus in the Morning. 6

Fairest Lord Jesus 8

Take My Life and Let It Be 10

Glory Be to The Father. 11

While By the Sheep 12

Swing Low, Sweet Chariot. 14

In The Cross of Christ I Glory 16

Go Down, Moses 17

America. 18

Every Time I Feel The Spirit 20

Now Thank We All Our God 22

Christ The Lord is Risen Today 24

Amen. 26

Standin' in the Need of Prayer 28

Joshua Fought the Battle of Jericho 30

Rejoice, Ye Pure in Heart 32

Music Dictionary 33

Saviour, Like a Shepherd Lead Us

Text — attr. Dorothy A. Thrupp
Tune — William B. Bradbury

Je - sus, Bless - ed Je - sus, Thou hast bought us, Thine we

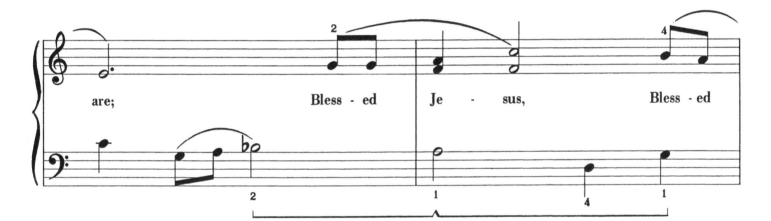

are; Bless - ed Je - sus, Bless - ed

Je - sus, Thou hast bought us, Thine we are.

2. We are Thine, do Thou befriend us,
   Be the Guardian of our way;
   Keep Thy flock from sin defend us,
   Seek us when we go astray.
   Blessed Jesus, Blessed Jesus,
   Hear Thy children when they pray;
   Blessed Jesus, Blessed Jesus,
   Hear Thy children when they pray.

3. Early let us seek Thy favor,
   Early let us do Thy will;
   Blessed Lord and only Saviour,
   With Thy love our bosoms fill.
   Blessed Jesus, Blessed Jesus,
   Thou hast loved us, love us still;
   Blessed Jesus, Blessed Jesus,
   Thou hast loved us, love us still.

Jesus in the Morning

Traditional

With a joyful swing

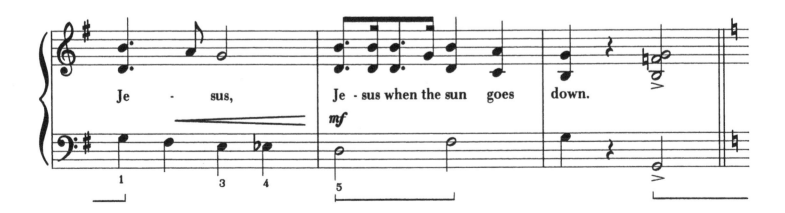

Fairest Lord Jesus

Text — German, 17th Century
Tune — Silesian Folksong

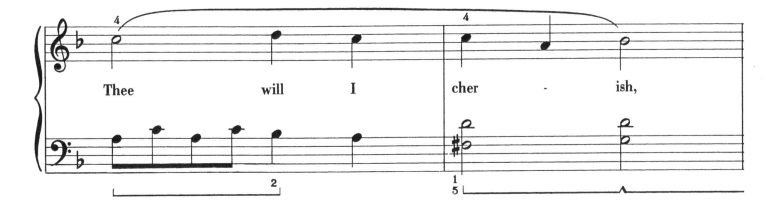

Thee will I cher - ish,

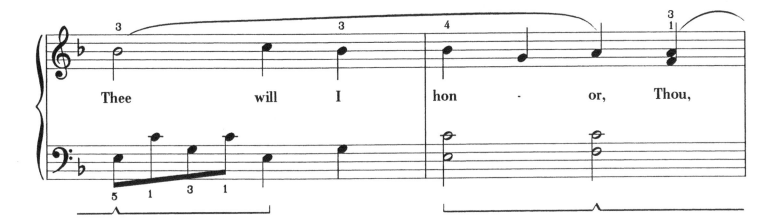

Thee will I hon - or, Thou,

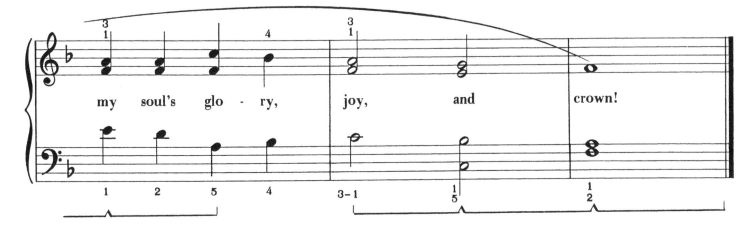

my soul's glo - ry, joy, and crown!

2. Fair are the meadows,
   Fairer still the woodlands,
   Robed in the blooming garb of spring;
   Jesus is fairer, Jesus is purer,
   Who makes the woeful heart to sing.

3. Fair is the sunshine,
   Fairer still the moon light,
   And all the twinkling starry host;
   Jesus shines brighter, Jesus shines purer
   Than all the angels heaven can boast!

4. Beautiful Savior!
   Lord of the nations!
   Son of God and Son of Man!
   Glory and honor, Praise, adoration,
   Now and forever more be thine!

Take My Life and Let It Be

Text — Frances Havergal
Tune — Cesar Malan

Glory Be to The Father

Text — Traditional
Tune — W. H. Greatorex

With spirit

Glo - ry be to the Fa - ther, and to the
Son, and to the Ho - ly Ghost; as it
was in the be - gin - ning, is now and ev - er shall be,
world with - out end. A - men, A - men.

While By the Sheep

Text — Traditional
Tune — German Melody

With gladness

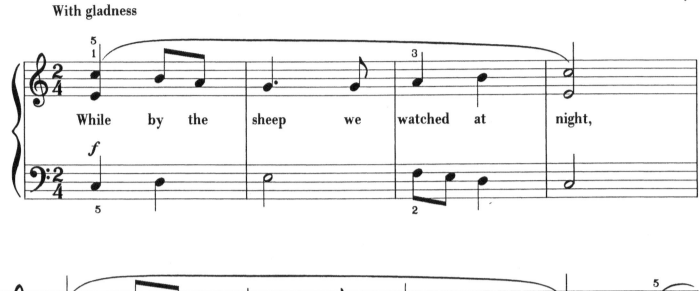

While by the sheep we watched at night,

Glad tid - ings brought an an - gel bright! How

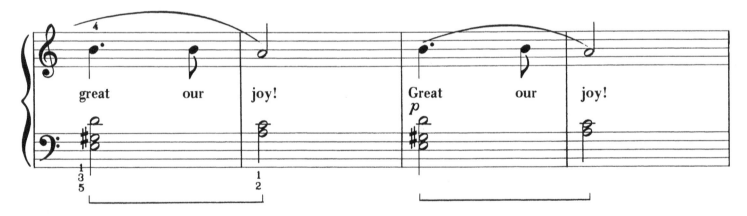

great our joy! Great our joy!

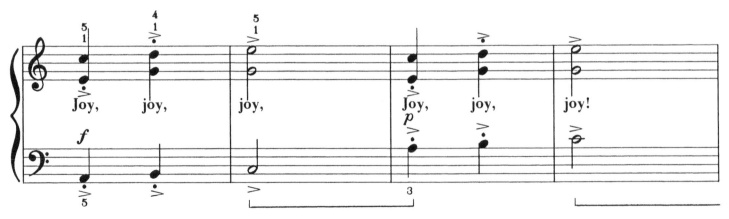

Joy, joy, joy, Joy, joy, joy!

Praise we the Lord in heav'n on high!

f

Praise we the Lord in heav'n on high!

p

rit.

Swing Low, Sweet Chariot

Traditional

looked o - ver Jor - dan, and what did I see

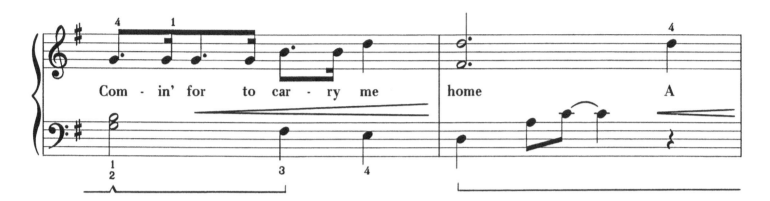

Com - in' for to car - ry me home A

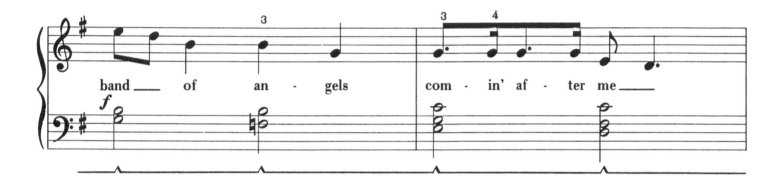

band ___ of an - gels com - in' af - ter me ___

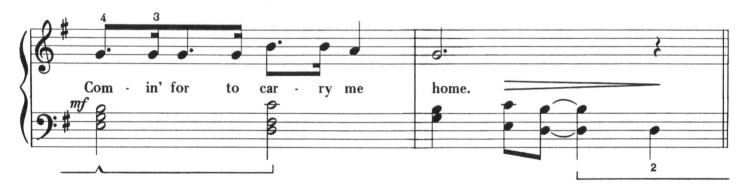

Com - in' for to car - ry me home.

Very slowly

In The Cross of Christ I Glory

Text — John Bowring
Tune — Ithamar Conkey

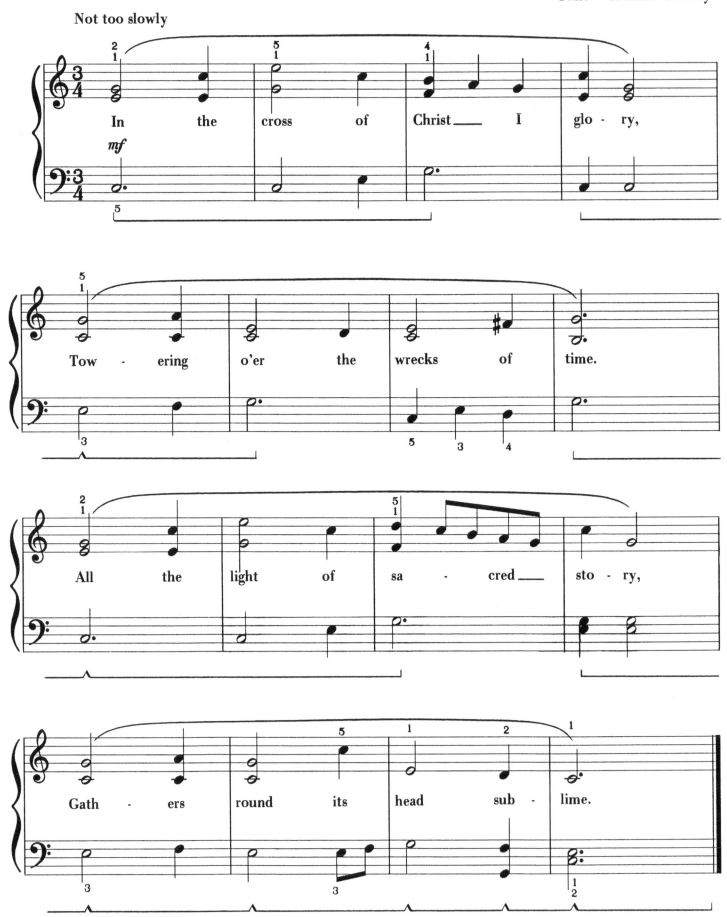

Go Down, Moses

Traditional

America

Text — Katharine Lee Bates
Tune — Samuel Ward

Joyfully, with dignity

shed His grace on thee, And

crown thy good with broth - er - hood From

sea to shin - ing sea!

2. O beautiful for pilgrim feet,
   Whose stern, impassioned stress
   A thoroughfare for freedom beat
   Across the wilderness!
   America! America!
   God mend thine every flaw,
   Confirm thy soul in self-control,
   Thy liberty in law!

3. O beautiful for heroes proved
   In liberating strife,
   Who more than self their country loved,
   And mercy more than life!
   America! America!
   May God thy gold refine,
   Till all success be nobleness,
   And every gain divine!

4. O beautiful for patriot dream
   That sees beyond the years
   Thine alabaster cities gleam
   Undimmed by human tears!
   America! America!
   God shed his grace on thee,
   And crown thy good with brotherhood
   From sea to shining sea!

Every Time I Feel The Spirit

Traditional

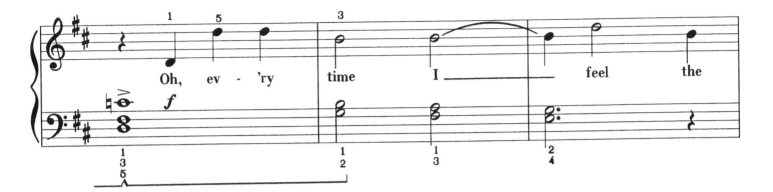

Oh, ev - 'ry time I _____ feel the

spir - it _____ mov - in' in my heart, _____ I will

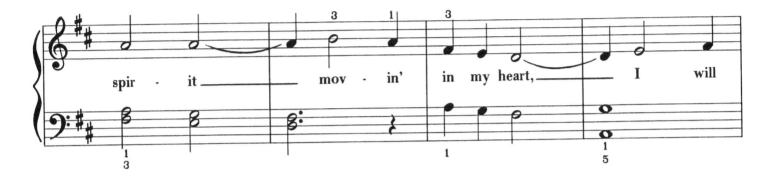

pray. Yes, ev - 'ry time I _____ feel the

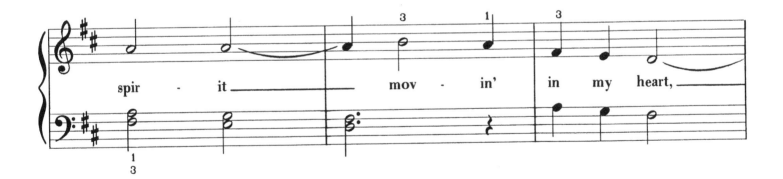

spir - it _____ mov - in' in my heart, _____

_____ I will pray.

Now Thank We All Our God

Text — Martin Rinkart
trans. Catherine Winkworth
Tune — Johann Crüger

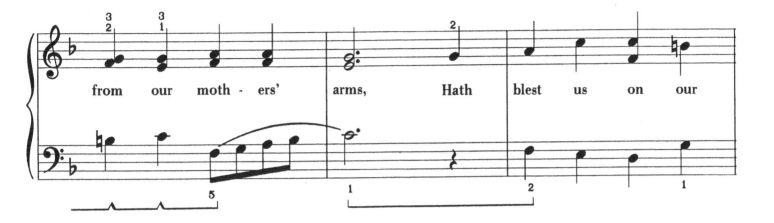

from our moth-ers' arms, Hath blest us on our

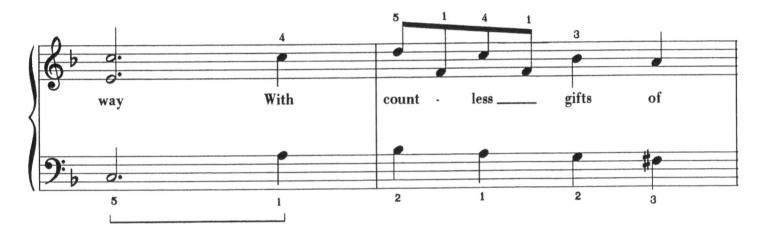

way With count - less _____ gifts of

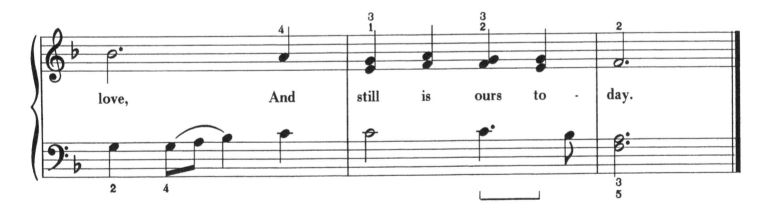

love, And still is ours to - day.

2. O may this bounteous God
   Through all our life be near us,
   With ever joyful hearts
   And blessed peace to cheer us;
   To keep up in His grace,
   And guide us when perplexed,
   And free us from all ills
   In this world and the next.

3. All praise and thanks to God,
   The Father, now be given,
   The Son, and Him who reigns
   With them in highest heaven,
   The One Eternal God,
   Whom earth and heaven adore;
   For thus it was, is now,
   And shall be evermore.

Christ The Lord is Risen Today

Text — Charles Wesley
Tune — *Lyra Davidica*, 1708

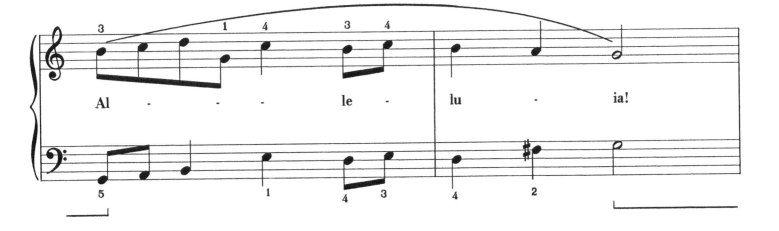

Al - - - le - lu - ia!

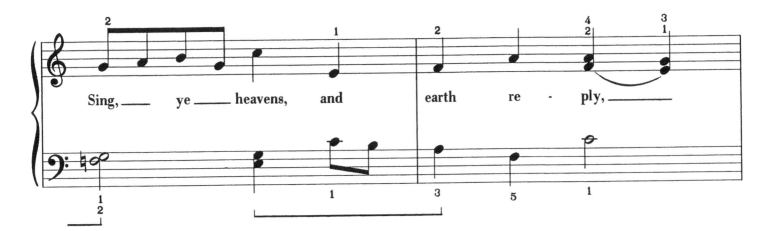

Sing, —— ye —— heavens, and earth re - ply, ——

Al - - le - lu - ia!

rit.

2. **Lives again our glorious King,**
   Alleluia!
   Where, O death, is now thy sting?
   Alleluia!
   Once He died, our souls to save,
   Where's thy victory, O grave?
   Alleluia!

3. **Loves's redeeming work is done,**
   Alleluia!
   Fought the fight, the battle won,
   Alleluia!
   Death in vain forbids Him rise,
   Christ has opened Paradise,
   Alleluia!

Amen

Traditional

With a lively swing

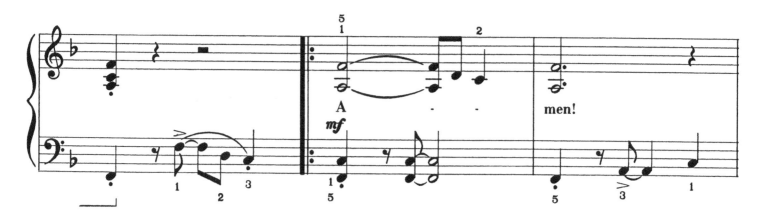

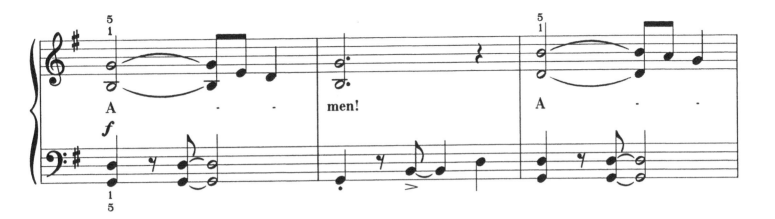

Standin' in the Need of Prayer

Traditional

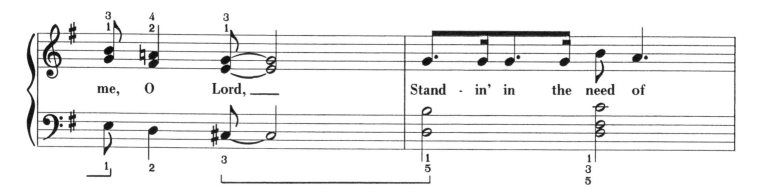

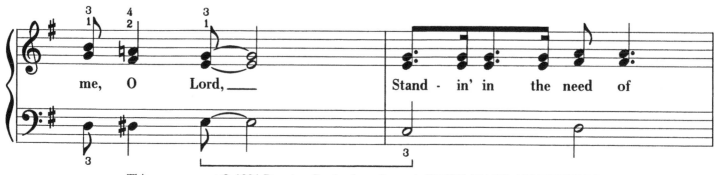

prayer, Not my sis - ter, not my broth-er, but it's me, O Lord, __

Stand-in' in the need of prayer. It's me, O Lord, It's __

me, O Lord, __ Stand - in' in the need of prayer. It's

me, O Lord, It's __ me, O Lord, __ Stand -in' in the need of,

echo   **Slower**

Stand-in' in the need of prayer.

Joshua Fought the Battle of Jericho

Traditional

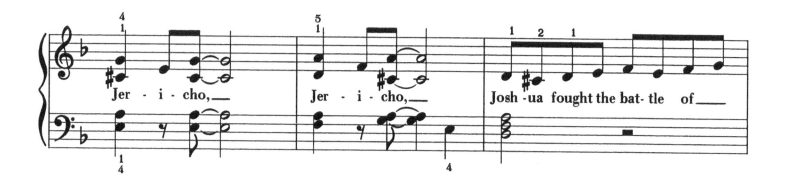

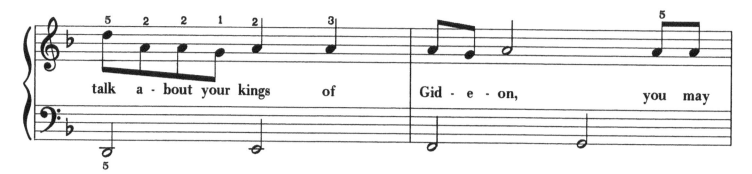

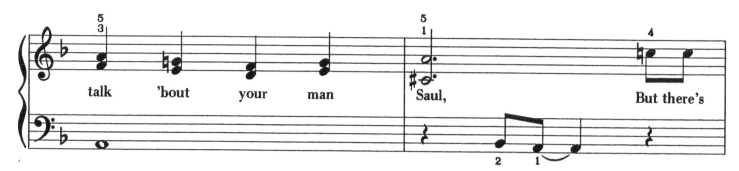

This arrangement © 1991 Dovetree Productions, Inc., c/o FABER PIANO ADVENTURES.
International Copyright Secured.   All Rights Reserved.

none like good old___ Josh - ua, at the bat - tle of Jer - i -

cho. Josh - ua fought the bat - tle of___

Jer - i - cho,___ Jer - i - cho,___ Jer - i - cho___

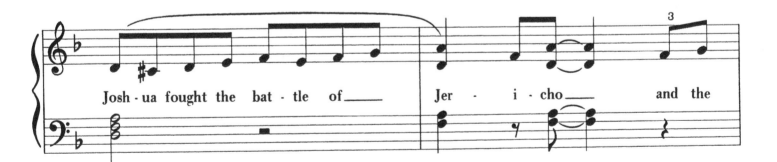

Josh - ua fought the bat - tle of___ Jer - i - cho___ and the

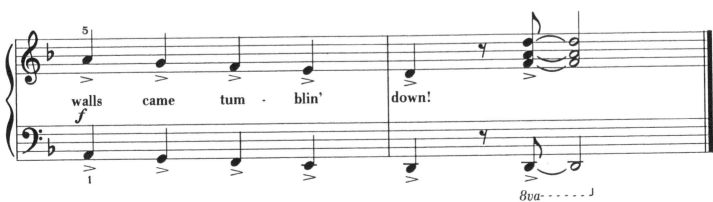

walls came tum - blin' down!

8va- - - - - -

Rejoice, Ye Pure in Heart

Text — Edward H. Plumptre
Tune — Arthur H. Messiter

Joyfully

Re - joice, ye___ pure in heart, Re - joice, give___ thanks and

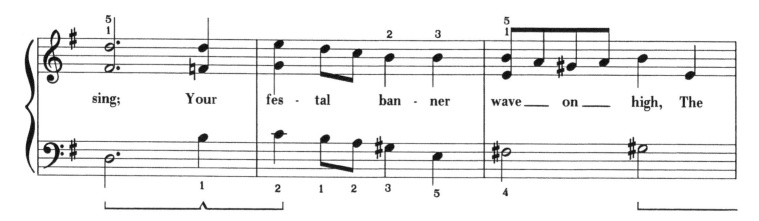

sing; Your fes - tal ban - ner wave___ on___ high, The

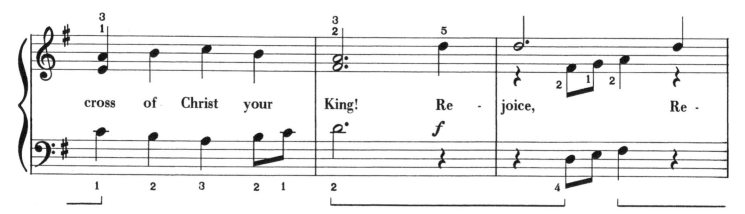

cross of Christ your King! Re - joice, Re -

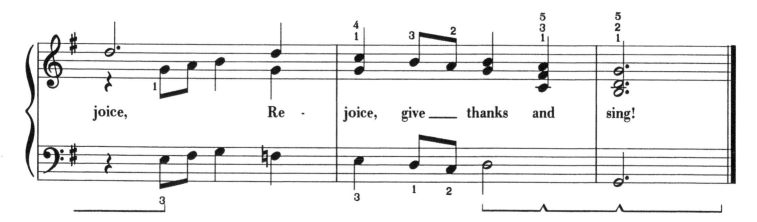

joice, Re - joice, give___ thanks and sing!